Heather Hillenbrand
Soul Fire Productions ISE PLLC
hrhillenbrand@gmail.com
heather@scottsdalesextherapy.com
www.soulfireprod.com
www.agirlsmagic.com

Special Thanks to George and Shelley Cambanes, Sharon Moloney, Wasim Moughaouiche, Tony and Noel Jordan, and Marc and Leif Rempel.

© Copyright 2022 Heather Hillenbrand. All Rights Reserved. No part of this document may be reproduced or transmitted in any form or by any means, electronic, mechanical, photocopying, recording, or otherwise, without prior written permission of Heather Hillenbrand.
ISBN # 978-1-7328688-4-7 Registration # 2022914470
Published by Heather Hillenbrand PO Box 31551 Phoenix, AZ 85046

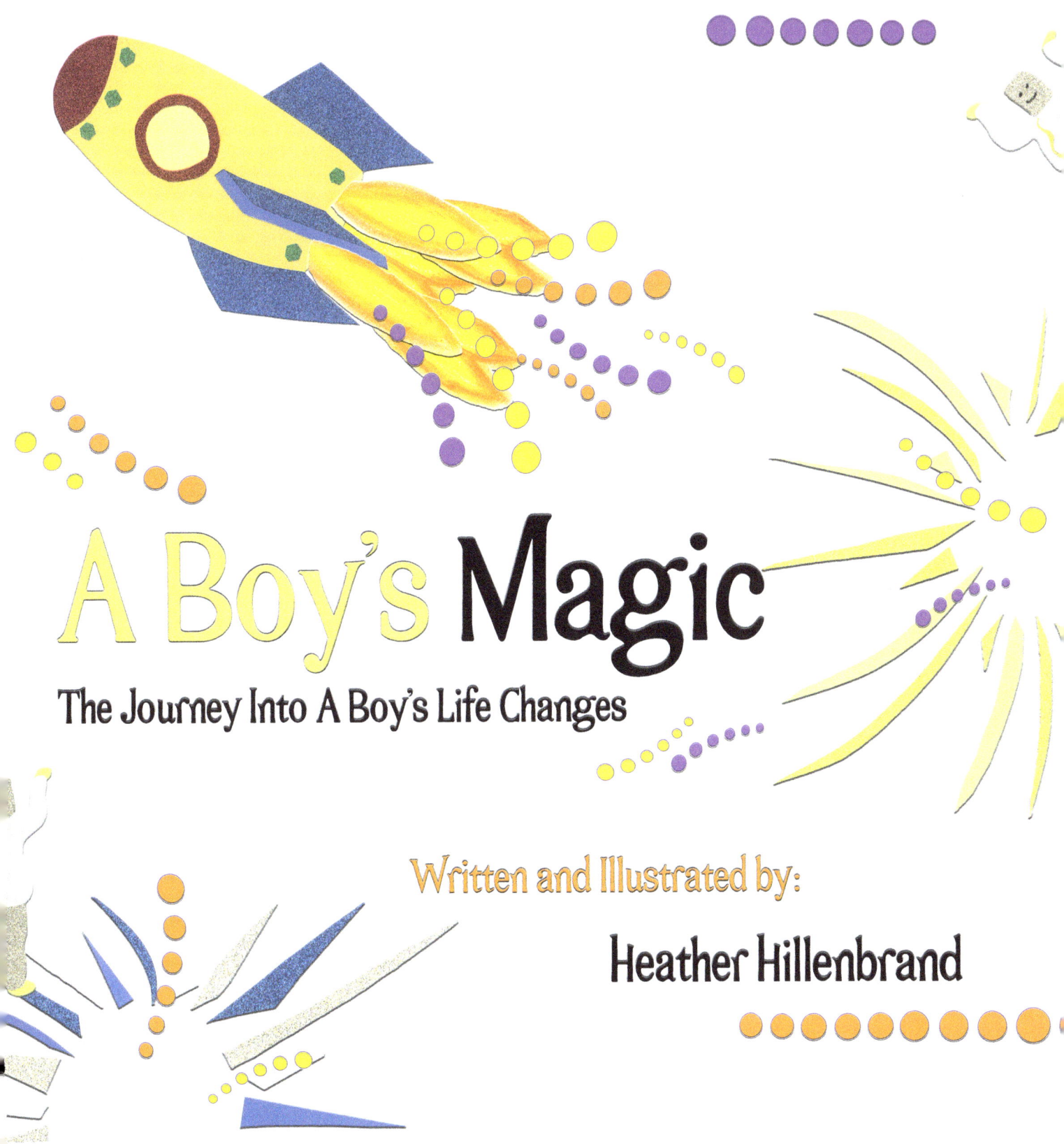

This book is dedicated to my sweet nephews Zach, Justin, and Evan. May your lives be rich with love and pleasure!

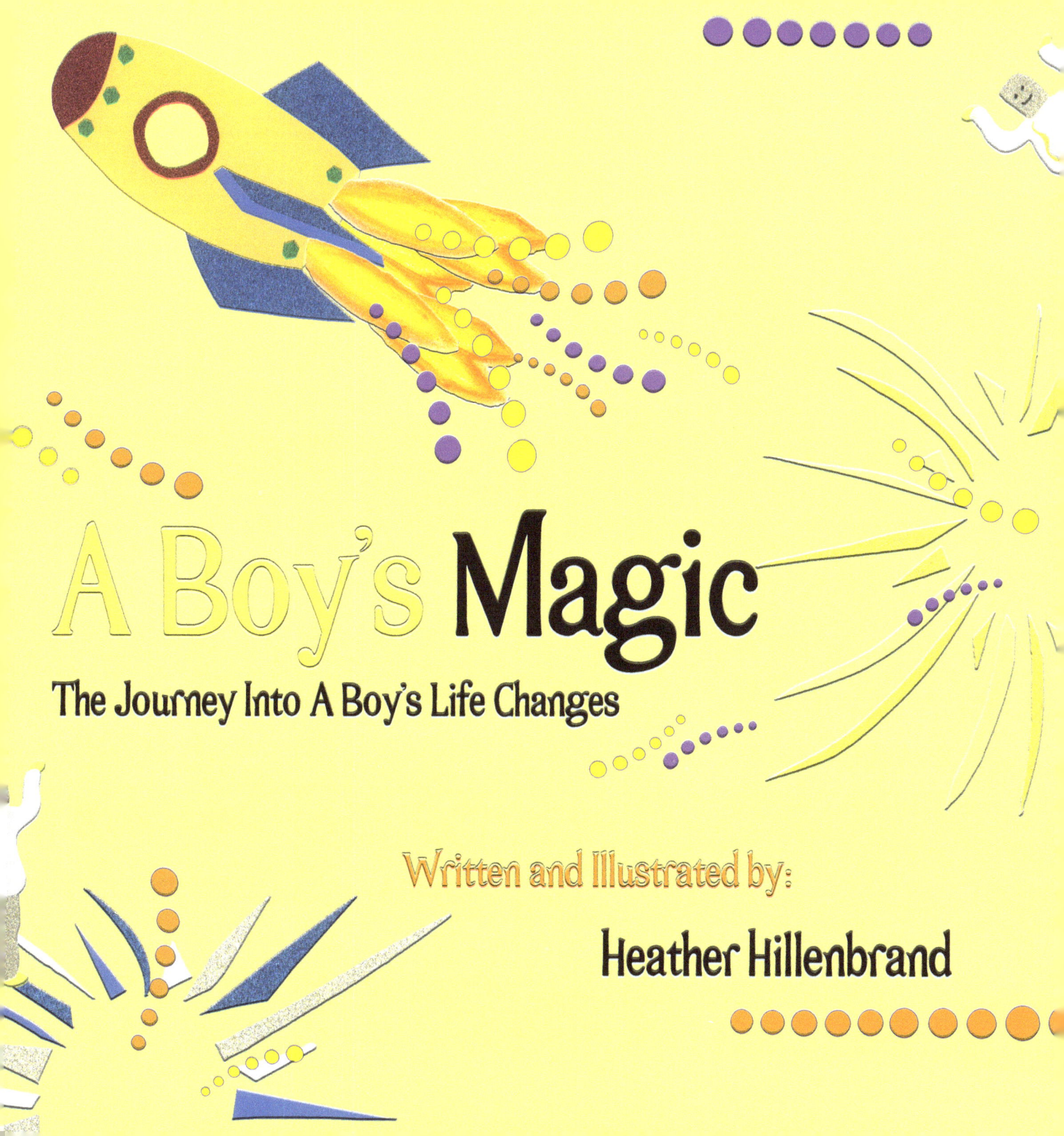

A Boy's Magic
The Journey Into A Boy's Life Changes

Written and Illustrated by:

Heather Hillenbrand

Every boy has a special magic...
Including YOU!

This magic is a powerful magic.
It started with your Father's spark
That's what helped to create you!

A boy's magic flickers from the Sun, lighting the way for imaginings that come alive from the fun of being.

A boy's magic shoots him through his Mama.
He is born with just an ember.
This ember grows, shines,
and inspires all who see.
There is no hiding his light...

Because a boy's magic burns so Brightly!

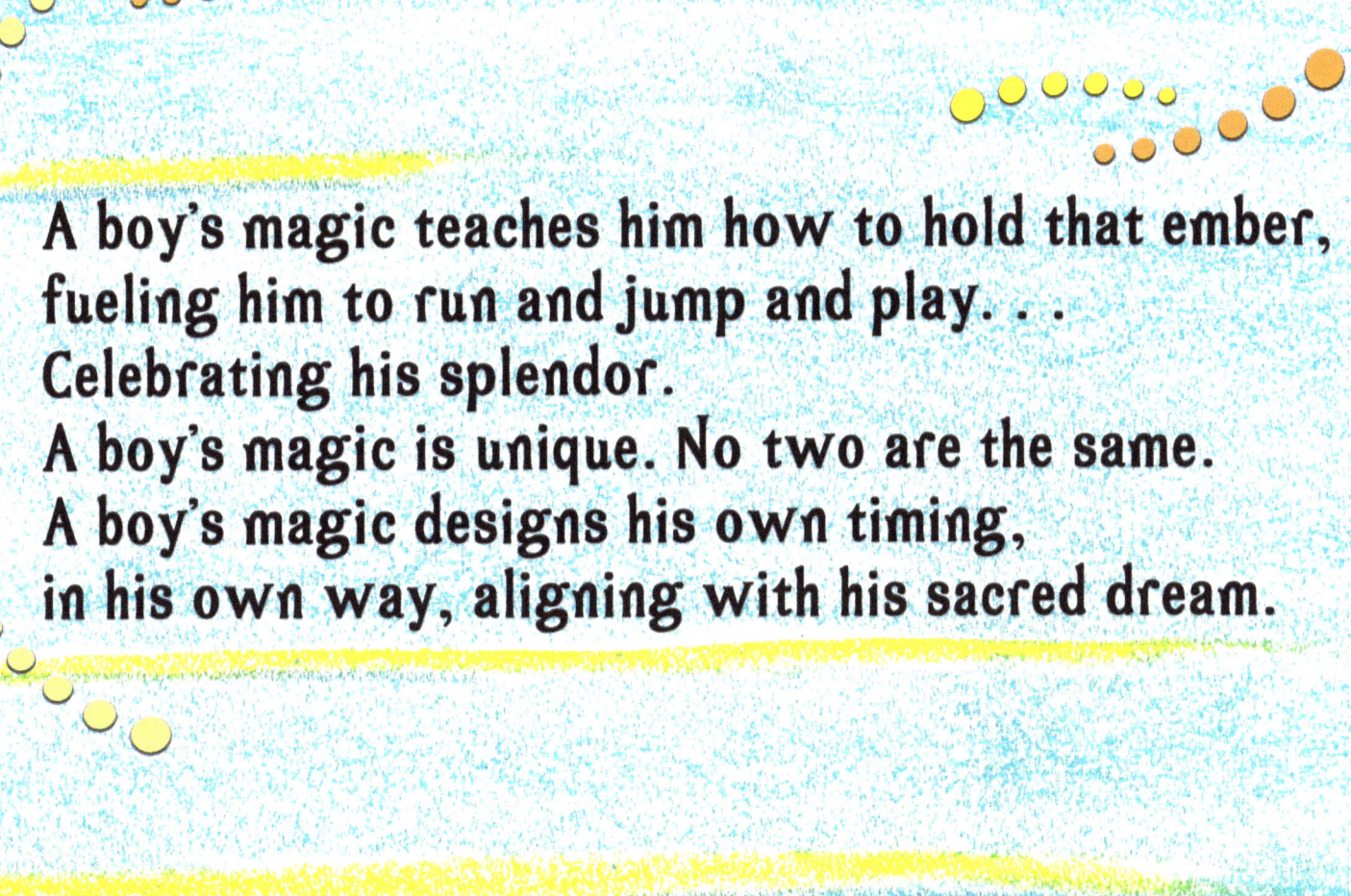

A boy's magic teaches him how to hold that ember,
fueling him to run and jump and play. . .
Celebrating his splendor.
A boy's magic is unique. No two are the same.
A boy's magic designs his own timing,
in his own way, aligning with his sacred dream.

When his ember turns to a spark,
It wakes him up to who he will be.

Strong and *wild* and free,
He embraces his instincts, learning
When to stop and when to go
How to love or take it slow.

A boy's magic is sometimes Rough and Tumble
With slingshots and rocks,
Playing biceps games of glory!

It also teaches him to be gentle,
Knowing how to tell his story,
Realizing how strong tenderness can be.

A boy's magic constructs buildings of safety and
Rockets of joy.
Forges fortresses of abundance,
Conjures castles of confidence.
A Boy's magic is cooperation.
Generating embers in the dark night,
He joins together armies for the light.

A boy's magic helps him grow...
Sometimes fast, sometimes slow.
He gets taller and sturdier.
He sprouts bigger feet, a wider nose while so
Much more grows.

But not always in that order . . .

A boy's magic happens in his own timing
Deciding when and where and
Which things to show.

Then one day...
A boy's magic transforms his body!
It turns his spark into the seeds of creation,
Sometimes called semen.
They come from his testicles and penis
Which grow and shrink with pleasure.

His semen allows the determination and inspiration
For babies, dreams, and many other beautiful things.

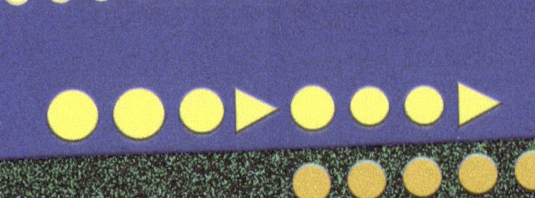

Maybe hair will show . . .

On his face and other places,
Sometimes patchy or bushy,
Sometimes not at all.

Each boy's magic is different from the next.
He can be short or tall, big or small. . .

But his size doesn't matter.
It's his kindness, wisdom,
Heart, and humor that
Makes him greater.

A boy's magic stands up for what is right!
He gives respect and honesty to those he loves.

A boy's magic deserves honor,
Knowing he has the power to spark life,
and bring about changes through strife.
A boy's magic creates and shines with pride,
Knowing he can be the spark and the light in the night.

His sparks are now seeds
That protect and provide beauty,
Building starships of his ability.

A boy's magic brings skill to his body,
Teaching him to be careful and
Aware of how he is powerful.

These changes are normal and natural,
Creating each boy originally his own,
Getting him ready for his creativity to be grown.
A boy's magic can happen overnight
in a flash of unknown. . .

So new and unique,
A boy never wants to come down!
A boy's magic sparks the beginning of change
Becoming the stars in the universe
Seeding his hopes and dreams.

After this *extraordinary* moment, a boy's magic is forever changed. He is new and different. *Nothing is the same!*

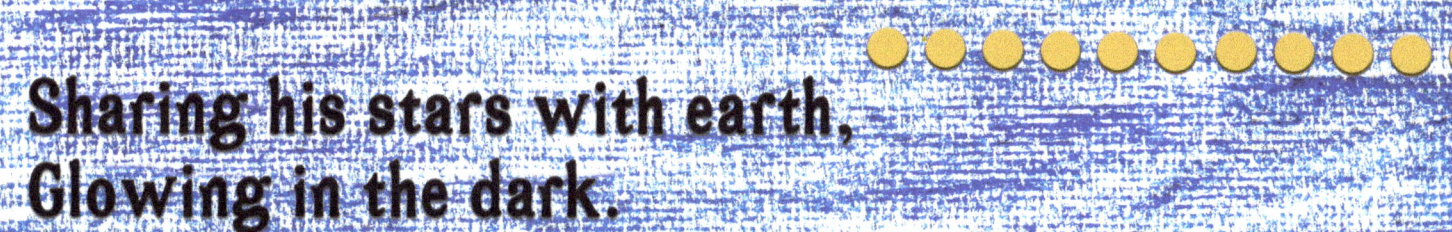

Sharing his stars with earth,
Glowing in the dark.
Providing his spark,
He illuminates the ADVENTURE life has to offer!

A boy's magic is the journey he
Takes to becoming a man.
Things are different and new
and it is certainly true,
This magic launches him to
Exactly who he is meant to be. . .

Parent Guide

A Boy's Magic helps parents teach the connection to the sacredness of puberty and budding sexuality. Embracing and celebrating a boy's physical changes as a Rite of Passage during his formative years imparts self-love, self-acceptance, and self-esteem. These concepts build confidence; empowering boys at a young age. Here are some simple things to keep in mind when talking with your son.

Communicating Thoughtfully

- When your son or loved one asks questions, answer them freely with a neutral, confident demeanor. It is important to mask surprise, shock, or even denial as these reactions may non-verbally communicate negativity about the questions asked.

- If you are not ready to answer a question, you could say, "That is a good question and I want to answer you the best way I can! I need a little time to think about it. Can we discuss it later? Set a time to discuss the question asked within three days. Ignoring it or waiting too long could also send a negative impression about the topic.

- When questions about sex arise at a young age, we tend to be shocked - not knowing how to respond. But this is an important part of life! Answer these questions with something like this: "That is a very big question with a lot to explain and I want to teach it to you. Let's start with your changes first." Allow A Boy's Magic to guide you in this endeavor.

Be Courageous

This book answers the question, "But how do I tell him about the other stuff?" Teaching about reproductive anatomy is far different from teaching about the many other changes that occur including feelings of pleasure. The key here is to know it is a process. Take your time. Read the book then return to it for a deeper dive into a specific topic. Remember, it is natural. Be brave and know you are chartering new territory for parents everywhere! For more clues on how to use this book and talk to your kids about sex, visit www.soulfireprod.com or email Heather at hrhillenbrand@gmail.com.

About the Author

Heather Hillenbrand, LAMFT provides sex educational or therapeutic support to parents, adolescents, couples, and individuals. As a Sex and Relationship Therapist, she holds a Master's of Advanced Study in Marriage and Family Therapy from Arizona State University and a graduate level Human Sexuality Certificate from the University of Minnesota. Heather offers therapy for couples and individuals at the Scottsdale Center for Sex and Relationship Therapy. She also facilitates sex education workshops and classes. Her company, Soul Fire Productions, hosts the many offerings as well as the creation of books and other sex education tools. She believes it is each person's birth rite to have knowledge and freedom of expression regarding sex, sexuality, and relationship. For more information, contact Heather at www.soulfireprod.com or email her at hrhillenbrand@gmail.com.